Jesus'
secrets
Revealed

WINNING
AT LIFE

Reality Check Series

REALITY CHECK | SIX DISCUSSIONS

Jesus'
secrets
Revealed

WINNING
AT LIFE

MARK ASHTON

WILLOW CREEK RESOURCES

ZONDERVAN™

GRAND RAPIDS, MICHIGAN 49530 USA

ZONDERVAN™

Winning at Life

Copyright © 2002 by Willow Creek Association

Requests for information should be addressed to:

Zondervan, *Grand Rapids, Michigan 49530*

ISBN: 0-310-24525-7

Interior design by Sherri L. Hoffman

Printed in the United States of America

02 03 04 05 06 07 08 /❖ CH/ 10 9 8 7 6 5 4 3 2

To Caleb,
a lover of Jesus stories.
May his Story always define your life.

CONTENTS

THE POWER OF STORY

I love a good story, don't you?

There's just something about it that satisfies both mind and heart. Since the beginnings of human community, stories have been used to bond people together, explain behavioral principles, and give meaning to life.

We're surrounded by stories in all forms—books, television, movies, songs, the Internet. But the best-known stories of human history are actually stories that Jesus told while he walked on the earth.

Surprised?

Jesus' illustrative tales (also called parables) were used for many purposes: to blast through the stereotypes of his day, expose religious hypocrisy, illuminate minds to spiritual truth, and inspire people to win at life—by living Jesus' way.

Jesus was no boring storyteller either. His anecdotes were masterful—verbal dynamite that blasted through the stone-cold hearts of his detractors. They also provided highly memorable pictures for his followers. Snapshots of truth so strong that many of his followers traveled the world retelling those stories.

But you might be wondering, aren't Jesus' stories old—told for his day only, so long ago? Why should you bother to study what he said after all those years?

The answer is simple: because the very stories he told affect your understanding of yourself, your priorities, your relationships with people and God, and your response in times of crisis and stress.

In his stories Jesus used heroes, people groups, occupations, and practices that would be well-known to his audience. Yet because he lived in first-century Palestine, these same illustrations are much less familiar to audiences two thousand years later—and on the other side of the globe. For that reason we've updated the stories, placing them in a modern-day context, to give them the same illustrative force they had in Jesus' day. But the primary message—and the impact—is the same.

In this guide, every discussion of Jesus' stories begins with an Icebreaker—a question or two that will stimulate your thoughts and also make it easy for you to share your ideas and opinions, even with people you may not know very well or at all. You'll read words from the Bible that reveal the purpose of Jesus' stories and then have the opportunity to discuss them with others. Each topic ends with a Reality Check—a few questions that will help you apply what you've learned to your own "story." And in the back of the book is a story you won't want to miss: "A Surprising Penalty."

As you find answers for your own life, you'll get a bonus too. You'll not only discover the power and value of Jesus' stories, you'll also discover fascinating things about Jesus himself—and the way he responded to people. You'll become aware of the power of money and how to keep it in perspective. You'll uncover the secret of reducing anxiety in your life. You'll wrestle with the spiritual barriers that keep people from optimizing their spiritual life—and learn the keys to overcoming them. You'll meet a hero nobody would have expected (even more, Jesus held him up on a pedestal!). As you internalize these stories, they will mark your life and help you chart a course to experience life at its best.

ROLLOVER INVESTMENTS

ICEBREAKER

Think about the magazines you are likely to find in a grocery store line or a bookstore magazine rack. How do magazines like *Glamour, Sports Illustrated, GQ, Maxim,* or *Cosmopolitan* answer the question, "What is valuable?"

Justify your answers with articles, quotes, pictures, or ads.

Looks
money
fame
winning

Read Luke 12:22 – 34

Then Jesus said to his disciples: "Therefore I tell you, do not worry about your life, what you will eat; or about your body, what you will wear. Life is more than food, and the body more than clothes. Consider the ravens: They do not sow or reap, they have no storeroom or barn; yet God feeds them. And how much more valuable you are than birds! Who of you by worrying can add a single hour to his life? Since you cannot do this very little thing, why do you worry about the rest?

"Consider how the lilies grow. They do not labor or spin. Yet I tell you, not even Solomon in all his splendor was dressed like one of these. If that is how God clothes the grass of the field, which is here today, and tomorrow is thrown into the fire, how much more will he clothe you, O you of little faith! And do not set your heart on what you will eat or drink; do not worry about it. For the pagan world runs after all such things, and your Father knows that you need them. But seek his kingdom, and these things will be given to you as well.

"Do not be afraid, little flock, for your Father has been pleased to give you the kingdom. Sell your possessions and give to the poor. Provide purses for yourselves that will not wear out, a treasure in heaven that will not be exhausted, where no thief comes near and no moth destroys. For where your treasure is, there your heart will be also."

DISCUSS!

1. Jesus tells his followers not to worry about life's mundane needs. Look back at the things the magazines consider valuable. How could valuing these things cause worry?

— peer pressure   — materialistic focus

2. Contrast the magazines' message with Jesus' message.

don't worry about the things that aren't important

3. What is valuable according to Jesus' teaching—and do you think this is a realistic way to live?

4. In what ways are people similar to and different from the flowers and birds used as Jesus' examples?

— flower + birds are content
people are wanting more.

5. From Jesus' words and your own experience, how do you imagine one might gain "treasure in heaven"?

— personal relationship with god

Jesus' final statement, "for where your treasure is, there your heart will be also," is illustrated well in a story Jesus told to a greedy man.

Story (adapted from Luke 12)

Daniel Mulligan was an investing genius. In the mid '80s, he joined a tiny software firm that was about to hit it big. They paid him a decent salary with great stock options. By the time he cashed them in, Daniel was a multimillionaire. He continued working as an executive for the firm, carefully investing and growing his cash.

Sara Mulligan married Daniel just out of college. She stuck with him through years of seventy-hour workweeks and bore him two beautiful children — now 15 and 17. Daniel was a good provider, but wasn't home much. When he was, he spent most of his time on the computer, surfing sites like investwithme.com. Just like he was doing tonight.

By this time in their life and marriage, Sara didn't mind so much. She'd lived this way for years, and she was used to it. But tonight was different. Soon their life together would change. Over the years, Daniel had made enough money to allow them to live in luxury off the interest. Next month he would retire, and they could begin living the life they always wanted!

Sara and Daniel looked forward to traveling, reading, and spending time with the kids. "As soon as life slows down," they had always said, "we can care for the poor, visit our families, and do the significant thing we have always dreamed of." All their lives they had wanted to become more spiritual people, but the time at work never allowed for it. Next month would be different.

As usual, Sara went to bed while Daniel was still working on the computer. Like many other nights, she awoke about 3 A.M. with nobody at her side. Knowing she'd find her husband asleep at his desk, she slipped down the stairs to rouse him. Sure enough, she found him slumped over his computer . . . but tonight something was different. When she touched his shoulder, he was cold and his arm fell limp to his side. His skin was clammy, and he didn't awaken at her voice.

Above his lifeless body, the computer read "disconnected by invest-withme.com."

When the paramedic arrived, he told Sara that Daniel had died of a massive heart attack.

At his memorial service, people lauded his friendly demeanor, business savvy, and hard work ethic. But that night, at his gravesite, an angel of God had another adjective that best described him — expressed as he traced his finger over the tombstone, carefully and slowly tracing the letters F-O-O-L.*

DISCUSS!

6. What's the sobering point of this story?

life is too short

7. What characteristics of Daniel or Sara do you recognize in people you know?

*Adapted from a message by John Ortberg, "It All Goes Back in the Box," given at Willow Creek Community Church, October 2000.

REALITY CHECK

Experts say that the best two indicators of your real priorities are your checkbook and appointment book or Palm Pilot. If someone else browsed your calendar and finances, what would they say your priorities are, and why?

One of Jesus' primary keys to winning at life is getting your priorities straight. How closely do your real priorities match up with what you want them to be? How well do they match up with God's priorities?

FOUR KINDS OF DIRT

ICEBREAKER

Tell a story you remember hearing as a child. Why do you remember this story so vividly?

Grandfather + 2 great uncles — Navy WWII
—shipped out to sea at some time.

What kind of impact—if any—has this story had on your life today?

- family sticking together - wives all lived together w/kids
- sacrifices

Jesus often used stories as a teaching device. They were highly memorable ways that his followers (from the educated elite to small children) could remember his teachings. Today we'll look at why Jesus used stories—and what we can learn from one of his most famous stories.

Story (adapted from Luke 8)

When a large crowd from many towns gathered around Jesus, he told them this story:

"A man built a house in a brand-new subdivision. He went out to his yard to plant his lawn by scattering grass seed. Some of the seed fell on the sidewalk, where it was walked on and eaten by the birds. Other seed fell into the gravelly soil near the street. It sprang up quickly, but soon died under the heat of the sun. Some seed fell among the crabgrass and dandelions. It came up, but was soon choked out by the weeds. Finally some of the grass landed on good, rich soil. It produced a rich, thick lawn — deep green and soft to the touch."

After Jesus told this story, he cried out, "May everyone who wishes to comprehend this story, understand it well."

The disciples, Jesus' closest followers, asked him what this story meant. He told them, "The secret of God's kingdom has been given to you! To others I use analogies and stories because just like in the time of Isaiah [a prophet who lived long before Jesus came to earth]:

"Those who see may not perceive and those who hear may not understand.'

"Here is the meaning of the parable: The seed is God's word. People are the four kinds of dirt. Sidewalk people are those with cement hearts. As soon as God's word comes, it bounces off of them and the evil one snatches it away so they will not believe it. Gravel people are the ones who respond to the word with joy at first, but fall away when trials come — because they have no roots. The weedy dirt stands for people who hear and respond to the word of God. However, their spiritual fervor is choked out by life's worries, love of money, or pleasure. These people never mature. The good soil represents people with noble and good hearts. They hear the word, retain it, and even through trials, grow to maturity."

DISCUSS!

1. The best way to figure out Jesus' storytelling technique is to evaluate the seed in each type of soil. Fill out the following chart as a group:

Soil Type	What Happens to the Seed	Type of Person Represented
Cement	walked on and eaten by the birds	
Gravel	_no roots	
Weedy	grows but choked out by others distraction	
Good	grows strong deeply rooted	

2. Why do you think some might understand Jesus' story, while others remain confused?

hard heart vs. soft heart

3. In the ending analysis, some of the best "dirt" in history were the lives of the disciples who followed Jesus. What was different about the disciples' response as compared to the rest of the crowd? (In other words, why has the knowledge of the secrets of the kingdom of God been given to them and not to others?)

—they are strongly committed to follow Jesus.

4. In light of the different responses people have to God's Word, why do you think Jesus used stories as such a key teaching tool?

- easy to remember

- stories were truth

5. Consider the soil that falls on the sidewalk. How is God's spiritual seed snatched away from people's lives today?

noise   wired world

6. The seed that fell in the gravel springs up fast and dies. Think of someone you know who has had a short-lived "religious experience." Why didn't it last?

7. The third group of seed fell among the weeds. As you look at our contemporary culture, what are some of the worries and preoccupations that can squelch spiritual growth?

REALITY CHECK

What type of soil would you consider yourself to be, and why?

gravel soil to weedy soil much of my life

One of Jesus' keys to winning at life was being open-minded and receptive to his own words. As we continue on this six-week journey of understanding some of Jesus' best stories, what can you do to be more receptive to understanding God's Word?

___ Come to this group with an open mind
___ Ask hard questions of the leader and the Bible
___ Reread the stories or other words from the Bible outside of group time
___ Pray daily that God will give a good understanding of his truth
___ Other _____

AN UNEXPECTED HOMECOMING

ICEBREAKER

Describe a place that feels like home to you. What makes you feel so comfortable there?

Story (adapted from Luke 15)

The following adaptation is based on the most famous story Jesus ever told (placed in a twenty-first-century context). In this story, he was talking to the religious elite, who were complaining because Jesus related warmly to "sinners" and even ate with them.

Scene One

Narrator: Priscilla hopped on the bus going south from the University of Illinois in Champaign to her home near Carbondale. Since the bus was mostly full, she scooted in a seat next to Lynn, a girl about her age who seemed lost in thought. After making an awkward introduction, and telling how much she loved her home, Priscilla began to ask where Lynn was going. Lynn reluctantly told why she wasn't sure if she'd go home or not after arriving in her hometown.

Lynn: I was raised on a farm about twenty minutes south of here, in Tuscola. My dad was a good man, a hard worker, and had only one dream for my older sister Elizabeth and me: that we would be the first in the Raczinski family to get college degrees. My sister did just as Dad said, but I was lured by the lights and glamour of Broadway. My dad had been saving all my life for my college education, but I got angry every time we discussed my future. After all, shouldn't it have been mine to choose? One day, in the midst of a big fight, I told my dad he was "just a stupid farmer" and stormed out. I took the money he'd set aside for my college and left. I haven't talked to him in two years.

Priscilla: No correspondence at all?

Lynn: I dropped a letter or two to Mom, just to let her know I was all right, but I didn't send anything to Dad.

Priscilla: How was life in New York?

Lynn: At first it was good. I had money and time. I went to lots of auditions and lots of parties — trying to connect with the Broadway elite. Unfortunately, there were hundreds of girls at every audition and I was never the one called back. Eventually my tuition money ran out.

Priscilla: I'm so sorry. . . .

Lynn: It gets worse. My part-time waitressing never paid the bills, and I wound up resorting to some, well, "unsavory" behavior to make the rent — if you know what I mean. After a while I came to my senses and decided to see if I could start over at home — even as one of my Dad's farmhands.

Priscilla: Wow. Do your parents know you're coming home?

Lynn: About a week ago I sent a letter to my mom. I told her to ask Dad if I could come home. If I'd be welcome back, the signal is to hang a towel out my old bedroom window. I can see it from the bus. If there is a towel, I'll go home.

Priscilla: And if not?

Lynn: I guess I'll ride the bus until they kick me off. . . . It's just around the corner here . . . I can't even look.

Priscilla: Wow! I don't know if this is your house or not, but it must be! There are towels hanging out every window. Sheets are on the trees and draped on the roof! Your dad must really want you home!

Narrator: Lynn excitedly tells the driver to stop, hops off the bus, and finds her dad running down the driveway to greet her. Teary-eyed, he grabs her in his arms, and holds her while crying, "My lost daughter is home!" "My dead daughter is alive!"

Scene Two

Narrator: Two hours later there's a party in the house. Neighbors and farmhands are coming over, food is abundant, and music is loud. Elizabeth comes back from a long day in the field. She is tired and sweaty, and refuses to go into the party. Her father comes out to talk with her.

Dad: Sweetheart, why don't you come in to the party?

Elizabeth: I can't believe you'd even have a party for that betraying, money-wasting daughter of yours! All my life I have done what you wanted — and you never even let me have a small party with my friends. Now this little wretch comes home and you invite the whole town!

Dad: Oh, my beautiful Elizabeth. In our home I am always with you. We always have each other, and everything I have is yours. But we need to celebrate because your sister was dead and now is alive. She was lost and now is found!

DISCUSS!

1. How would you feel if you were the father and Lynn asked for her money?

2. Why do you think Lynn came to her senses?

3. How would your own father have responded to you if you did what Lynn did and came home looking for mercy?

4. Is the reaction of the father surprising when you think about what Lynn has done to him—why or why not?

5. How would you feel if you were Lynn and you got this kind of reception?

6. Put yourself in the older sister's shoes. How would you respond if your "money-wasting sister" came home?

7. This classic story is an allegory about how God treats people who are far from him as well as people who are pretty moral. What does it say about God's heart?

8. Given that Jesus is telling this story to the moral-religious elite of his day, what's so shocking about the ending?

9. What does the father (both the one in the story and the heavenly Father) do that is similar for both daughters? What is different?

REALITY CHECK

Which character do you most identify with in the story? Why?

In order to "win at life" you must be fully connected to the heavenly Father. Both daughters always have an open door to enter a relationship with their father, but they have different barriers. What would it take for you to "come home" to the heavenly Father represented by the earthly father in this story?

WARNING SIGNS

ICEBREAKER

Describe the two best things about your workplace or the school you attend.

Imagine this is your workplace. Every day you go to work here. . .

www.efn.org/~hkrieger

Now imagine it's 7:30 A.M. You have just parked your car and a man runs up to you. He shows you this picture, telling you that by noon, your workplace will look like this:

www.corbis.com

Would you believe him, or continue on into work, and why?

What would it take for you to trust his credibility?

Story (adapted from Luke 16)

There was a man named Rich, who lived in luxury. He owned a mansion in an exclusive part of the city, drove a Porsche, hired in-home help, and dressed in fine clothes.

Just outside his gate lived a homeless man named Lazarus. He had multiple diseases and foraged through Rich's trash to find food.

The time came when the homeless man died. The angels carried him to heaven, where he was placed next to Abraham (one of God's most faithful servants).

Rich also died and was buried. He was taken to hell, where he was in torment. Then he looked up and saw Abraham far away, with

Lazarus by his side. So he called to him, "Abraham, have mercy on me and send Lazarus to dip his finger in water and cool my tongue. I'm in agony in this fire!"

But Abraham replied, "Rich, in your lifetime you received your good things, while Lazarus received the hard things. But now he is comforted here and you are in agony. Not only is your request inappropriate, but impossible, for there is a great chasm between us that cannot be crossed."

Rich pleaded, "Then please send Lazarus to my family. Have him warn my five brothers so they won't wind up tormented here with me."

Abraham replied, "They have heard the teachings of Moses and all of the prophets. Let them listen to them."

"No, Abraham," Rich said, "they may not listen. But if someone from the dead goes to them, they will repent."

"If they don't listen to Moses and the prophets," Abraham said calmly, "they won't be persuaded even if someone rises from the dead."

DISCUSS!

1. Contrast the lives of Rich and Lazarus before and after death.

2. What can clearly be known about their eternal destinations— and what is not clear?

3. In this story Jesus spoke of hell and warned people of the reality of our eternal destiny. Do you think it was mean or judgmental of him to do so? Why or why not?

4. Rich makes two requests—first, for personal relief, and second, to help his family avoid this destiny. Do these seem like reasonable desires of a person in hell? Why or why not?

5. What kind of requests would you make if you were in Rich's situation?

6. Abraham said people wouldn't even believe if they saw somebody rise from the dead. Here, Jesus was alluding not only to the story of the rich man and the poor man, but to his own historical resurrection. Do you think he was right? Why or why not?

REALITY CHECK

Just like the man warning of the terrorists attacking the World Trade Center, Jesus warned us of a day when we would be judged. The ultimate way to win at life is to beat death—and to be justified on Judgement Day. Jesus wanted us to be ready for the eternal consequences of this moment.

In your opinion, is Jesus a credible source? Why or why not?

What would it take for you to believe his warning?

LAME EXCUSES

ICEBREAKER

Describe the last time you were invited to a dinner or a party and you said no, though you actually could have gone. What excuse did you give, and why?

Story (adapted from Luke 14)

Caleb Gregovich struck it rich in the bottled-water craze of the '90s. He was a pillar in his community and well-regarded among business colleagues. He prepared a massive banquet for his friends, colleagues, and employees to celebrate the company's twenty-fifth anniversary. He sent out his executive team to personally invite each of his associates to the lavish feast.

But each of the associates began to make excuses.

The first said, "I have just bought a new piece of land where I can build my dream home, and I must go see it. Please excuse me."

Another said, "I just bought a brand-new car and I need to take it out for a drive. Please excuse me."

Still another said, "I just got married. So I can't come."

When the executives came back and reported this to their boss, Mr. Gregovich became very angry. He told his team, "Go back into town *and make sure everybody has received an invitation. Invite the homeless, the abused, people from nursing homes and hospitals. . . . Anywhere you find people, invite them!"*

They told him, "We already did that, and there's still room for more."

Then Mr. Gregovich said, "Then go to the surrounding towns and the farms. Invite people until my house is full! I tell you that not one of those people who rejected my invitation will get one taste of my banquet."

DISCUSS!

1. In this story, who does Caleb Gregovich represent?

Jesus

2. What is the party—and Mr. Gregovich's goal for the party?

— *participate in his glory*

— *share the joy of success*

3. How would you feel if you were Mr. Gregovich and you heard the excuses these people made?

— *hurt*   — *bummed out*

4. What are some excuses people in the twenty-first century make to not be a part of God's party?

— it's not for me
— with all the bad things in the world how can you believe?

5. Do you think these excuses are legitimate? Why or why not?

6. Jesus tells this story at a dinner party full of religious leaders who are devoted to their religion. In fact, the main reason they'd invited Jesus to the party was to see if they could trap him. Why do you think this story would shock his audience?

7. The last statement of the story was, "I tell you that not one of those people who rejected my invitation will get one taste of my banquet." What do you think this means?

If you deny God you will not taste the glory of heaven.

Read Luke 13:25 – 27

In a similar situation, Jesus said of heaven,

> *"Once the owner of the house gets up and closes the door, you will stand outside knocking and pleading, 'Sir, open the door for us.'*
> *"But he will answer, 'I don't know you or where you come from.'*
> *'Then you will say, 'We ate and drank with you, and you taught in our streets.'*
> *"But he will reply, ' I don't know you or where you come from. Away from me, all you evildoers!'"*

DISCUSS!

8. According to Jesus, who will make it inside the door and who might be left outside?

9. What reasons do people today give for why they should get into heaven?

I'm a good person.
Add up good + bad + if good outweighs bad

10. Are these reasons legitimate, according to Jesus? Why or why not?

REALITY CHECK

Jesus clearly taught that the greatest way to win at life is to know him and spend eternity at his party. If you haven't yet accepted God's party invitation, what things keep you at arms' length?

How might you overcome these barriers and get to know Jesus?

If you have accepted God's party invitation, what practical things are you doing now to grow in your intimacy with Jesus?

small group

How else could you get to know him even better?

- read more of the bible
- talk more to God
- take advantage of service opportunities

UNLIKELY HERO

ICEBREAKER

What's the closest you have ever come to a 911 emergency (seeing one happen, calling one in, watching the aftermath)? Tell the story. . . .

How did you and the people around you respond?

Story (adapted from Luke 10)

As Jesus was teaching one day, he was stopped by some religious lawyers who wanted to test him. "Of all of the Bible's laws, which is the greatest?"

Jesus queried, "What does your law say?"

One of the lawyers knew it by heart. "The greatest is this — 'Love the Lord your God with all your heart and all your soul and all your mind and all your strength.' The second greatest command is similar — 'Love your neighbor as yourself.'"

"You have spoken well!" Jesus told him. "Do this and you will live."

But in order to justify the depth of his question, the lawyer retorted, "Then, who is my neighbor?"

And Jesus told him a story, which, in the twenty-first century may have gone like this:

"Ernest Johnson, a Caucasian businessman, was returning from a business trip at 2 A.M., driving north on I-94 when his 'engine overheat' light came on. He was forced to exit into a part of Chicago's South Side known for its violence. Pulling over to the side of a dimly lit road, he got out of the car to look at his engine. A minute later a group of teenagers attacked him, beat him up, stole his wallet, slashed his tires, and left him for dead.

"Although the night was dark, it was easy for passersby to see the mangled body on the side of the road. Within thirty minutes, dozens of people saw the body and continued driving.

"Father O'Shaunessey was coming home from a round of hospital visitation. He saw the body, but was tired from a long day of ministry. So he changed lanes and went around the body, traveling home for his rest.

"Matthew Cheney, an elder at the Bible Church, was driving home after a long visit with friends. When he saw the body on the side of the road, he feared the same gang might threaten his own life if he stopped. Thinking of his waiting wife and kids, he decided he'd pull over and call 911 from his cell phone as soon as he got into a safe neighborhood.

"Carlos Lopez, a Hispanic immigrant and an atheist, was driving home after finishing a shift as a bouncer at the local strip club. Seeing the battered Caucasian man on the side of the road, he risked his life to pull over and help the man. Bringing a first-aid kit out of his trunk, he administered all of the care he knew how. He then hoisted Johnson, still unconscious, into his car and drove him to St. Andrews Medical Center emergency room. To the hospital staff this unconscious man, who had no ID, no family, and no money, was just another beat-up 'John Doe.' So upon his arrival, Lopez gave the hospital staff the cash he had in his wallet and his credit card — offering to pay for the man's entire care if, for some reason, Johnson's insurance didn't come through.

"Then, leaving Johnson in the care of the health professionals, Lopez finished his drive home."

After Jesus completed this story, he asked the lawyer, "Which of these three do you think was the neighbor?"

The lawyer responded, "Lopez — the one who had mercy on him."

"Then go and do likewise," Jesus wisely said.

DISCUSS!

1. Imagine you are the one driving through the worst part of the city and you come upon such a scene. In what ways would you identify with the priest?

2. What about the elder?

3. What would you have done, and why?

4. Why was Lopez an unlikely hero?

5. Jesus told this story in response to the question, "Who is my neighbor?" If you were to give an answer to this question in the form of a principle that summarized Jesus' story, what would it be?

6. If every person loved God and his or her neighbor the way Jesus taught, what would such a society look like?

7. Jesus' expectations for his followers were radical in terms of the love they were to extend. Some people find it very attractive, while others think it might be incredibly difficult. How might living this kind of a radical, love-filled life in the midst of a pain-filled world affect you personally?

REALITY CHECK

One of the key ways Jesus taught us to win at life is to love unlikely people. All of us are surrounded by "neighbors" we ignore, for various reasons. These people may be of a different race, different economic strata, different faith. They may have difficult personalities or be uncomfortable to be around. Or any other number of things. As you look around, who are the "neighbors" you may have been ignoring?

Jesus taught that you win at life by giving love away. What's one way you could love an unlikely candidate this week?

Jesus' expectations of his disciples are some of the highest in history. He wanted people who would live for him, love for him, and even die for him. On a scale of 1 to 10, where are you in terms of your readiness to follow Jesus in a complete, wholly devoted manner?

| 1 | 2 | 3 | 4 | 5 | 6 | 7 | 8 | 9 | 10 |

I like things
how they are

Where do I
sign up?

A SURPRISING PENALTY

Henry Iwashita and Doug Kono were friends from their toddler years. Raised in the same neighborhood, they were fast friends from preschool through their high school years. However, in their college years, they began to drift apart as they went to different colleges. At that point, their life paths diverged as well.

Doug completed college with high honors and went on to law school. After numerous years as a public defender, he was elected to be a judge, a position he faithfully held. He was noted as a fair, evenhanded judge who was meticulous about upholding the law.

Henry, on the other hand, dropped out of college soon after his father's early death. After trying and losing numerous jobs, he found himself frustrated at his lot in life. So he turned to a life of crime. He was a smart criminal, the perpetrator of a string of crimes so skillfully executed that he was never captured—or even suspected. By his late thirties, he was an expert at embezzlement and information theft via computer.

Then, to his chagrin, he was caught at age 39, trying to embezzle money and military secrets from his own state. Worse, when his computer was confiscated, it was linked to dozens of other formerly unsolved crimes. The evidence was clear, and the sentence for his treason was mandatory—death.

At his trial, Henry Iwashita found himself face-to-face with a fair, evenhanded judge who was meticulous about the law—his boyhood friend, Doug Kono. Henry expected leniency, but was met in the courtroom with the steady gaze of a clear-headed legal mastermind. If he didn't know better, Henry would have suspected this judge never had met him before.

Judge Kono efficiently managed the trial, weighing the evidence for Henry's guilt and his pending sentence.

Once the evidence was presented and the arguments were made, Judge Kono emerged from his quarters. He delivered the verdict: "The court finds you, Henry Iwashita, guilty of treason in the highest order. The mandatory sentence is death."

Then the countenance of the judge changed. He allowed all of the emotions of decades of friendship to emerge. His eyes filled with tears as he rose from the bench. "Further, my friend, I choose today to take your sentence upon myself. I will die so you may live and go free, with no further penalty to pay."

Judge Kono removed his robe, stepped down from the bench, and embraced his bewildered friend. For a moment they paused, weeping and holding one another. Then Judge Kono turned, held out his hands to be cuffed by the bailiff, and was removed from the courtroom. He, not Henry—who so deserved it—would face the sentence of death.

And that's exactly what Jesus, God's Son, did for us. All of us are like Henry Iwashita—we deserve the sentence of death for all of our wrongdoings, including the sin of deciding to turn away from God and go our own way. And yet God allowed Jesus to take our sins upon himself. Like Judge Kono in the story, Jesus chose to pay the death penalty on our behalf so we can live.

Jesus offers the gift of life freely. But it's up to you—and each one of us—to accept his "substitution" by choosing to accept that sacrifice on your behalf. If you want to do this, you just need to tell God. Choosing to accept this gift is as simple as ABC:

A. Admit you have done wrong that has hurt yourself, God, and others.

B. Believe that Jesus died on your behalf to pay for and forgive your wrongdoing.

C. Choose to follow Jesus with your whole life.

If you do so, you will be given the most wonderful gifts of all—a clean conscience, hope, purpose, and a fulfilling life with God not only now, but for all eternity!

LEADER'S GUIDE

INTRODUCTION

These discussion guides are unique. Whereas most Bible discussion guides are designed for devoted Christians, these are designed for people in all different places in their spiritual journeys. Some may be committed followers of Jesus. Others may feel far from God. You may have a group member or two who are committed to another faith. Some may have been raised in a churchgoing family, but drifted away later in life.

Having a mix of people with a variety of opinions will make your discussions much more lively. Newcomers to Jesus will benefit from the experience of veterans, while old-timers will begin to see Jesus with fresh eyes.

The focus of all the discussions will be the life and teachings of the most influential person in the history of the world—Jesus of Nazareth. You'll be observing him through the biographical sketches of eyewitnesses—people who were there, friends who knew him. This series assumes that participants have little or no knowledge of these biographies, or of the rest of the Bible. The Icebreakers, Read portions, Discuss! questions, and Reality Check applications are designed to be accessible, fun, and provocative for all people—regardless of their spiritual journey.

The overall guidelines for the discussion are simple:

- The format is discussion—no lectures or sermons allowed.
- The leader will not primarily be a teacher, but a question asker and participant.
- Everyone is encouraged to participate. It's assumed that all have something to offer . . . and something to learn!
- Everyone's opinion will be respected, but feel free to politely disagree—it makes for better conversation and learning.

- No prior knowledge or religious experience is required. A diversity of experiences will be valuable to the group.

Most of all, have fun!

HOW TO LEAD A GREAT DISCUSSION

Want to have a terrific group, with quality discussions? There are two simple principles: learn how to ask and use questions, and make sure you're prepared ahead of time.

The Power of Questions

The biggest key to quality discussion leadership is asking great questions. The questions in this guide will give you a good start to a fantastic discussion. But you'll have to go beyond these questions if you want to have the best kind of group. Here are some principles for excellence in question-asking.

Use the Icebreakers. These questions will be ones that people from all kinds of spiritual backgrounds will be able to answer. They are critical to warm up the atmosphere, develop affinity between members, and create a sense of "group." They are lighthearted and geared toward getting to know people. They also serve to set up the discussion topic of the day.

Ask open-ended questions. Questions that only have a yes, no, or one "right" answer are a dead end for discussion. Even questions that are observation driven should begin with phrases like "Describe, list, recount, imagine, compare, or picture . . ."

Don't settle for a single answer. Most of the questions in the guides are multifaceted and will elicit many responses. For the questions that invite a personal response—especially the Reality Check questions—encourage many (or all) of the people to answer. Ask the same questions in multiple ways if need be. If only one person answers, try this response: "That's helpful. What does somebody else think?"

Probe for answers that go beyond the surface. Ask people, "Where did you first hear that idea?" or "Have you always thought that, or have your ideas changed over the years?" or "Where did you see that in the passage?" You may want to reflect back people's responses by summarizing, "So what I hear you saying is . . ." Another way to go deeper is to simply say, "Tell me more about that." You'll be amazed at the depth of responses when you listen well and ask follow-up questions.

Finish with the Reality Check questions. These questions are designed to make the content personal, bringing factual discussion home and helping the group to identify with the passage personally. Some of the studies have multiple Reality Check questions. You may want to select one, try all of the questions, or wing it, depending on how the group responds to your first question.

Feel free to deviate from the guides. Sometimes a particular question will need to be rephrased to fit the people in your group. So change the question! A question may get answered in the course of discussion before you even ask it. Skip the question! Remember, your goal is to create a discussion around the person of Jesus. Use the questions to facilitate that goal, but don't feel bound by the questions. Be a good conversationalist. Build on what people are saying and use questions to keep them focused on the main point of the discussion. Sometimes God may lead you to set the guide and your preparation aside, and follow an important issue the discussion raised.

Preparing for the Study

Normally leaders would spend about two hours in preparation and prayer for this kind of discussion. About five to seven days before the group meets, go through the study and familiarize yourself with the Scripture verses. Focus particularly on the key topic of the study. Allow yourself to see Jesus with fresh eyes. Imagine how group members might react to him. Let the truth of the passage sink into your own life.

Spend the next week watching for personal connections—illustrations from your life, news stories that relate, magazine articles, or movie clips. Integrate these illustrations at appropriate moments in the study. Nuance the questions or even change the Icebreaker questions to fit what's currently going on in your life, the nation, our culture (be sure, though, that it stimulates fun conversation and relates to the topic at hand).

Then, the night before the group meets, spend another hour studying the Scripture passages and preparing questions. Imagine yourself in the flow of the conversation. Figure out how to help the group understand the key theme. Craft your questions to bring out the best possible group interaction, understanding of Jesus, and focus on that key theme.

Then relax—and enjoy the group!

Note: The numbered questions in Discuss! correspond directly to the numbered questions earlier in the guide. However, not all questions will have a corresponding Leader's Note—only the questions that may have more difficult answers or need more direction. For more information on leading great discussions, check out www.zondervan.com/realitycheckcentral.org.

DISCUSSION ONE

ROLLOVER INVESTMENTS

For your first meeting together, take a few minutes to meet one another. Find out names and other basic information, such as where people live or work. Then launch into the first Icebreaker.

In this discussion topic, group members will see the stark contrast between Jesus' values and the values of our culture. They'll also discover how closely connected worry is to our cultural values and, hopefully, how aligning themselves with Jesus' values is the wisest (and least anxiety-producing) way to live.

ICEBREAKER

The most blatant expression of cultural attitudes can be found in the checkout lines of supermarket aisles. *Cosmopolitan* and *Glamour* (for men, *Sports Illustrated, Maxim,* and *GQ*) don't try to hide behind any moral or highbrow veneer; they reflect what people think and want. Therefore they are a great source to find out what our culture values. Find a few copies of these magazines to bring with you to the group. Give group members plenty of time to answer the question, "What is valuable?" by studying the magazines.

Make sure you wait until they look beyond the obvious answers—money, prestige, sexual appeal, and clothing—to the less obvious physical characteristics of models, underlying prejudices, greed, or lust. Another critical value embodied in these magazines is the constant desire for more. Even the magazine itself promotes unrealistic models of success (consider that the models are the country's most beautiful women, perfectly made up, professionally lighted and posed—yet their imperfections still need to be airbrushed!).

Not only will this magazine discussion be fun, it's the perfect setup to contrast Jesus' teaching in Luke 12.

Note: If you don't have the actual physical magazines for the discussion, you can ask people for their memories and impressions of such magazines from seeing them in the grocery store or bookstore, etc.

Read Luke 12:22–34 • DISCUSS!

Question 1. After reading the passage, reconnect with your *Cosmo* list of values. Ask how those values produce worry. Group members may become sober, but that's all right. This should be a sobering moment, since such values affect all of our lives. Because they have already read the words of Scripture, they will be realizing the stark contrast of Jesus' values to those of our culture. Don't move to the question from the passage too fast, so that this contrast can be as strong as possible.

Questions 2–3. Make sure each group member sees the "worry-free, seek first the kingdom" values and connects them to Jesus' unique message. You may need to diverge a bit here to talk about God's worthiness of our trust and how confidence in a credible source reduces worry.

Question 4. God values birds and flowers, but—much more so—humans! God will watch out for our needs even more than those of the birds.

Question 5. Tell group members, "You are precious to God because you are eternal!" Focusing on God and people will lead to a life of greatly reduced worry. And who couldn't use less worry in their lives?

Story (adapted from Luke 12) • DISCUSS!

Question 6. Like most of Jesus' stories, the story of Daniel Mulligan has a single point. Amassing wealth is of no value once you die. It's amazing how many people go through life seeking security and prestige through finances, only to find that kind of life-focus empty once it's achieved.

Question 7. It's likely that group members will first realize— and talk about—these characteristics in others first, before they recognize it in themselves. But that's alright. It is more safe in your first discussion to focus on cultural problems in the third person, before you move to personal application. Go ahead and move on to the Reality Check once all group members understand the main point of Jesus' story.

REALITY CHECK

Using the checkbook and Palm Pilot as a benchmark helps people pinpoint their real priorities without weaseling an ambiguous answer out of them (either because they don't know or because they're embarrassed to say). The truth is that most of us fall short of our own standards for how we would like to spend our time and money. When it comes to God's standards, we are way behind.

Ask group members to think about this question over the next week: How much better would your quality of life (not to mention your eternity) be if you lived life with Jesus' priorities rather than by the shallow values promoted in *Glamour*? Applications will vary from things related to beauty, to money, to family, to worry. There is no "right answer" here. Allow people to disclose what they wish, and then affirm that sharing—without judgment or any expectation of receiving a certain answer.

FOUR KINDS OF DIRT

This discussion topic is designed to help people get in touch with their own particular openness (or lack thereof) to spiritual things. It will also help them gain a vision of how they can become more open—in concrete ways. The discussion all revolves around understanding Jesus' parable of the soils, analyzing the different kinds of soil, and identifying with a particular soil.

Your purpose is not to slot everyone into the "correct" kind of soil; it's to begin a dialogue about their spiritual condition in a non-judgmental, open atmosphere.

ICEBREAKER

People love to tell—and hear—stories, so let them talk. The length of the story isn't what matters. What's important is that group members begin to feel comfortable talking about their life and sharing their experiences in front of the group.

Story (adapted from Luke 8) • DISCUSS!

Question 1. Filling out the chart together is a fun way to do what could otherwise be repetitive observation. For larger groups, try a flip chart if you have one. Having one focus point can stimulate group interaction. But in the absence of a flip chart, the guides will do quite well.

Encourage people to study the story for the answers to the chart instead of making up whatever comes to mind. This will set the tone for the group, showing people that many answers can be easily found right in the text just read.

Question 2. It's important to note that Jesus' preference is for everyone to hear and understand his parables. But he knows that even in the audience he is speaking to, there are people who represent each kind of soil. Some will hear and walk away. Some will pursue further answers—and those are the ones who will know the secrets of God's kingdom.

Question 3. As you compare and contrast the disciples and the crowds, the difference is simple. The disciples asked further questions and pursued truth. The secrets of the kingdom of heaven are found by those who eagerly pursue reality and ask questions. Be sure your group understands that Jesus *valued* those tough questions and wanted people to find answers. He never asked them to blindly believe without understanding.

This has profound implications for your group. Like Jesus' followers, they should be free to ask hard questions! They should doubt, debate, and be skeptical at times. But their doubt and skepticism should be resulting from an intense quest for spiritual reality rather than because they want to ignore the tough issues and walk away in denial.

Question 4. Jesus used stories because their meaning, although always profound, is not always obvious. This story sorted out those who were eager for truth (question askers) and those who just wanted to bluff or pretend they understood.

Questions 5–7. As people examine the different kinds of soils, give them the freedom to speculate and tell stories about people, if they are so inclined. Jesus' story intersects our everyday reality so strongly here that it's helpful to see its direct implications two millennia after the first telling.

REALITY CHECK

Let the group express the state of their spiritual openness—and reasons for it—without any judgment in your facial expression, body language, or words. Most will be able to tell very clearly what kind of soil they think they are.

Most group members will also identify steps toward more openness. If you've done a good job of setting the pace of acceptance and safety, you may be surprised just how well people respond to this question.

AN UNEXPECTED HOMECOMING

This story from Luke 15 is perhaps the most beloved parable of God's amazing grace. In today's parable (as well as the two others in Luke 15), God's heart for people is exposed. The story shows how much he loves the lost one and constantly wants to bring the found one into his experience of rejoicing. Your discussion together will give group members great insights into the heart of the Father and the role of his children.

ICEBREAKER

As your group time begins, discuss the feeling of "home." Who doesn't long for it? Who can't identify with needing that kind of comfort? A warm kitchen, laughter, and the smell of baking brownies are such common experiences that it will create built-in affinity with your group. Putting group members on an even plane discussion-wise sets a wonderful, positive tone.

Story (adapted from Luke 15)

Each of the discussion topics in this book uses a different experiential device to aid the learning process (charts, magazines, photographs, movie clips, and, in this case, a drama). Encourage group members to take the roles of the different characters and read as though they were really the person in the drama. This will make the story stand out in significant ways—both during the group and afterwards. You will need a narrator and four players (Lynn, Priscilla, Elizabeth, and Dad). If you have less than five in the group, just have each person (except the narrator) do multiple parts.

DISCUSS!

Question 1. Imagine the sense of betrayal and loss that the father must have felt when his daughter wanted to leave his house, his dreams, and take his hard-earned money. Be sure group members get a sense of the offense of her departure.

Question 2. "Coming to her senses" was simply the obvious choice. She knew she would be better off at home than destitute in New York. But it took humility to make that decision. Some of your group members might be able to identify with this.

Question 3. After discussing the first few details of the story, you'll ask how group members' fathers may have reacted in this situation. This part of the discussion may be humorous, intense, or mundane, but it will certainly give you clues about people's varying backgrounds. Oftentimes people will impose their impressions of their earthly father onto the heavenly Father. And in today's dysfunctional world, these images are often negative. Such negative experiences with a dictatorial, verbally or physical abusive, or even emotionally absent father results in stained images of God that must be addressed in order for the person to have spiritual breakthroughs. Although it may or may not be wise to draw this out during the discussion (it depends on the type of group and the "emotional safety" within that group), the leader should watch for people's memories of their dads and consider how those experiences might affect their patterns of relating to God.

Questions 3–4. These questions are designed to give insight into the heart of the father—not only the earthly father in the story, but our heavenly Father. So be sure to dwell on this part for a while. The father's response here is nothing short of stunning. His love for his daughter runs deeper than his love for money, prestige, or his reputation in the community. He wants to restore her and celebrate her after a major betrayal. Why? Just because he's so gracious.

Question 5. As group members put themselves in Lynn's position in the story, they'll reveal their own experiences on their spiritual journey. Hopefully group members will come to this realization on their own: Knowing the Father's love makes it safe to run to him. Otherwise, they might need promptings such as, "Would the kind of father you're returning home to—a loving father versus an abusive father—make you want to come home sooner? Why?"

Question 6. In discussing this story, the ending is as notable as the beginning. Actually, Jesus' target audience (the Pharisees and teachers of the law) was represented by the older sister—aloof and disinterested in the new life of the "sinners" Jesus called his followers. The older sister's cold heart was exposed as it was contrasted with the warmth of the father.

Many people find it easier to identify with the older sister than with the younger. Perhaps it's because we all tend to be a little self-righteous in our attitudes at times—thinking we're better than other people who are more sinful than we are. But that kind of attitude serves only to alienate us from others, who may see us as haughty or judgmental, and from God, who looks at our hearts even more than our actions. Those who have truly experienced grace—especially from more radical circumstances—can oftentimes extend that grace more easily toward others.

Question 7. God's heart is one of love and compassion. He is not a respecter of persons. He treats all people, no matter their background or situation, equally.

Question 9. The father's attitude was the same toward both daughters. Although they were clearly in the wrong, he went out to them and invited them in to the party. Both had to learn about grace—from differing perspectives—and the father was willing to teach them. His love extended equally to the flagrant sinner and the self-righteous prude.

REALITY CHECK

As people check their own hearts by identifying with one of the sisters in the story, let them talk about their need to come home to God in the terms they see fit. Unless you've explained the gospel to group members (even in its simplest form), they may not understand that coming home in its fullest sense means trusting in Jesus' death on the cross for forgiveness—and then choosing to follow him in all his risen power.

Most group members will realize there are barriers between themselves and God. But they may not know how to move beyond these barriers. This might be a perfect time to show the group a good gospel outline, such as "A Surprising Penalty" in this guide. It will clarify the "homecoming" process in a way the parable cannot.

DISCUSSION FOUR

WARNING SIGNS

ICEBREAKER

Warning! This discussion topic may have strong shock value! The graphic images of the World Trade Center may bring up painful memories and strong emotions about the sin-tainted nature of the world. Members may have to face the concept of destruction— both temporal and eternal.

But isn't that exactly what Jesus did? He used strong images and graphic pictures to wake up his audience to the reality of eternity. Nobody in the Bible talked about hell more than Jesus. In fact, he talked more about hell than heaven. Why? Because he loved people. His love was so deep that he didn't want them to be separated from him. He wanted people to avoid that pain and know the true life that can be found only in him. He never avoided the truth—or its consequences. Just as Jesus shot straight with his audience, you must be clear with your group.

In the introductory segment, the main point is about warnings, not destruction. The idea here is not to parallel the destruction of the World Trade Center with the destruction of hell, but to parallel the warning of our imaginary messenger with the warning Jesus gives later in the passage.

Be sure not to spill the content of the story before people form their opinions of what makes the warning credible. You'll want to refer back to their standards later in the discussion when you evaluate whether to trust Jesus' warnings.

Story (adapted from Luke 16) • DISCUSS!

Question 1. This simple observation question will ease people into the passage. Obviously, before death Rich had it good, while Lazarus had it bad. After death, however, they switched places.

Question 2. Due to this story, group members may raise questions that cannot be answered. A member might ask, "Can people in hell really see the people in heaven?" Because this is a parable Jesus is telling and not a doctrinal description of hell, we really can't conclude this is exactly how hell will be. The nature of hell is really unknown from this passage—and not clearly described in any other passage. Be careful to stick to the main themes of the topic and not to wander too far into speculation about hell. If somebody asks a question that's not clearly answerable, just say so! People will respect your honesty.

What can be known from this passage, however, is that hell is awful. Rich is isolated and in agony while Lazarus is at peace in community (with Abraham). What's not clear is *why* each is in their final destiny. There is a correlation in this story between riches on earth and eternal rewards, but that doesn't mean that being poor means an automatic entry into heaven and vice versa. For instance, Abraham was fabulously wealthy and yet is in heaven.

This story of Jesus is silent on the subject of *how* to get to heaven. If group members are interested in this concept, you may want to point them to the "A Surprising Penalty" story in this guide—or take some time during the group to discuss it.

Question 3. In this instance, Jesus is warning his audience about the finality of heaven and hell (and alluding to his resurrection as the sign of his authority in this matter). He is similar to the person in the introductory segment who warned people about the bombing of the World Trade Center. If what he's saying is true, he isn't being mean and judgmental. As a matter of fact, telling people the truth about how to avoid a terrible future is the most loving and kind thing a person can do. Christians are often criticized for discussing eternal matters, but they too are being compassionate if they do it in others' best interests.

Question 4. One of the main reasons Jesus told this story is captured in the requests of Lazarus. First he asks for personal relief. His existence is miserable, and he wishes he could have just a little taste of water for his parched mouth. The next request is even more telling. He wants his relatives to avoid this destiny and *asks* for a warning from a credible source. An interesting sidelight to this story is the plausibility of this request. I can imagine that most people in hell would wish this for their loved ones.

However, one of the biggest emotional barriers that seekers of God's truth face when considering Christianity is the idea that loved ones who have passed away are in hell. Be very careful about this! This emotionally charged issue needs to be handled with a high degree of sensitivity. The truth is, however gracefully stated, that if friends or relatives are in hell, they would want those still living to avoid their same fate. If heaven and hell really do exist, everybody would want the living to make it into heaven.

Question 6. Abraham's statement, "They won't be persuaded even if someone rises from the dead," is also quite revealing. The real Lazarus in John 11 (not this fictional Lazarus) rose from the dead, and many people did not believe Jesus. As a matter of fact, some religious leaders responded by plotting to kill Jesus. Then Jesus himself rose from the dead, and yet many people didn't believe him!

REALITY CHECK

This segment of the discussion is particularly poignant. You may want to open this segment by recalling the standards of credibility raised for the person holding the World Trade Center photo. Did Jesus fulfill these standards? Is there anything he could possibly do to give him more credibility as a source of information about eternity?

For those in your group who are skeptical, this discussion should serve as a strong pointer to listen to Jesus carefully. Nobody before or since has predicted his own death and resurrection, then pulled it off! Because Jesus broke the death barrier—three days in the tomb—and came back to tell us about it, he is history's most credible source on life after death.

The stakes are sky-high, so it's imperative your group members understand the choice is theirs. A great way to finish your meeting is to reinforce this fact with a clip from the movie *The Matrix*—the scene where Neo and Morpheus meet for the first time. Morpheus presents Neo with a red pill and a blue pill and asks him to decide which one to take. End the clip as soon as Neo puts the pill in his mouth.

Then tell group members: "Like Morpheus in *The Matrix*, Jesus is only offering the truth. And like Neo, it's up to you to choose whom you will believe about spiritual reality."

DISCUSSION FIVE

LAME EXCUSES

This study is designed to help group members think through the excuses to joining God's party. They'll examine how valid those excuses really are and have the opportunity to consider what they might miss if they continue to believe those excuses.

ICEBREAKER

Because of the question, the group discussion will begin on a fun note. After all, the lame reasons people give to miss a date or a dinner party *are* pretty ridiculous. After the laughter, note that there seems to be a difference between the excuses people offer and the real reasons for not joining the party. This discrepancy may be useful to refer to later in the discussion.

Story (from Luke 14) • DISCUSS!

Question 1. In this story, Mr. Gregovich represents God.
Question 2. His party is heaven. More than anything else he wants his banquet to be full. He wants to throw a huge party and

watch people enjoy it. He isn't concerned with whether the people are high-class or low-class, or where they are from. The invitation is extended universally.

If group members (especially Jewish groups) are concerned with why Jesus kept extending the circles of invitation, the answer is found in his original audience. Jesus was speaking to Jewish leaders. He was telling them that the invitation to join God's family would be spread not only to God's people, the Jews, but to a wider and wider swath of people, including non-Jews (Gentiles). The invitation was to go out to all nations—in ever-widening circles. He was clearly communicating two things to his listeners: that more will be invited, and that the Jews who reject the invitation will be shut out.

Note: This, however, will not be the main point for a non-Jewish group. Most groups will be looking at the excuses people make and the consequences of their decisions.

Questions 4–5. Take plenty of time to brainstorm the excuses people make in our generation to not join God's party. They may be generic excuses—or ones group members use themselves. Either way, evaluate together the legitimacy of each excuse in light of eternity. As a leader, skillfully ask follow-up questions, such as: "Do you think that's the real reason? Or is it just a veneer for something deeper that's going on?"

Question 6. The shocker is that some of the people at this dinner party may wind up shut out of God's heavenly party! These people may have thought their place in heaven was secure because of their Jewish heritage, but Jesus tells them decidedly otherwise. The high-voltage tension at this moment would have reverberated through the room!

Question 7. Jesus makes it clear that the people must accept—rather than reject—his invitation. If not, they will be shut out! Some people might find this unfair and personally offensive. Others might take a serious spiritual inventory of their lives and listen closely to Jesus as a result.

After your group discusses this story, they will look at a passage with a similar point. The second passage (Luke 13:25–27), however, is more propositional teaching and less like a story.

Read Luke 13:25–27 • DISCUSS!

Question 8. Jesus tells people that those who "know him" will be inside the door. Others who heard his teaching will be left out. Even those who ate and drank with him could be left out.

Questions 9–10. People in your group may think they'll go to heaven because they heard the Bible taught in their homes. Perhaps they were raised in a Christian family and think that this has gained them admittance. Or maybe they even go to church regularly and are very moral. But it's clear from Jesus' words that he has no concerns for the externals. Those are not legitimate reasons to get into heaven from his perspective. Instead, it's the acceptance of Jesus' death on the cross for our sins and a subsequent choice to follow God's way instead of our own that opens the doors of heaven.

REALITY CHECK

The most important factor for this discussion topic is intimacy with Jesus. Ask group members, "Do you know Jesus—not just as a concept or a historical figure, but as a person?"

"Do you know Jesus?" will be the standard question asked of every soul on Judgment Day. Every person will cross the threshold of death and go either to heaven or hell, based on their answer!

This Reality Check portion simply takes the third-person concepts of this discussion topic and makes them personal.

"What things keep you at arms' length?" is a wonderful question that can open up worlds of deep spiritual conversation.

Some people may say they are ready to accept Jesus' invitation at that very moment. If so, help them to take the appropriate steps—either during group time or immediately after.

Others may still have significant barriers. Listen well to them and honor their openness. Then get on the solution side of their problems. Help them work through whatever issues they may have so they don't become spiritually stagnant.

For those who already clearly know Jesus, talk about the steps they can take to maintain and deepen their relationship. This will also help those not yet convinced in your group to see the ongoing process of a love relationship with Jesus, as opposed to a static, one-time commitment.

UNLIKELY HERO

This discussion is more about a transformed life than the process of finding God. For the spiritual seeker, it's a window to the life God wants us to have. For the believer, it's a model for ministry.

ICEBREAKER

There's nothing like a 911 emergency to get your heart pounding— or to show better how people respond. Some will tend to act quickly; others will be almost frozen, unable to act due to fear. The stories and people's responses in crisis will set a great stage for one of the best-known of Jesus' stories—the parable of the good Samaritan.

Story (adapted from Luke 10)

The merciful character in this story is so famous that many hospitals are named for him. "Good Samaritan" laws have been passed to protect people who make injurious mistakes in the act of trying to help a person. Yet often people's familiarity with the parable makes them dull to its cutting edge.

What's really happening in this story? Jesus is verbally slam-dunking the religious leaders who are asking the question, "Who is my neighbor?" You see, these leaders knew that loving God and people was the greatest commandment. But in trying to save face by trapping Jesus in a rhetorical battle, they actually opened them-selves up to one of the classic stories of all time. In addition to answering their question, Jesus addresses their racist and religious prejudices, confronting them with their own ugliness.

DISCUSS!

Questions 1–3. In the retelling of this parable, modern-day par-allels are brought to bear on the story. Most Westerners don't understand ancient Jewish culture and racism, but they can quickly recognize it in our own society.

The response of the priest and elder—to ignore the battered man's crisis—is what humans would normally do. All of us primarily consider our own best interests, rather than those of a stranger. If your group doesn't seem to understand this more extreme scenario, try asking these questions: "Have you ever passed up someone else's need because it wasn't convenient for you? When, and why?" or "Have you ever needed something, but someone refused to help you because it wasn't convenient for him or her? What happened, and how did you feel about it?"

Question 4. As the conversation turns toward Lopez, be sure the group notes that he is a minority (someone the Jewish leaders of Jesus' day would consider the scum of the earth) and an atheist—the kind of person Jesus' audience would least expect to risk his life to give roadside help. That's why the story is so shocking. After all, the irreligious outcast is more moral than the two Christian leaders!

Oftentimes people who investigate Christianity are looking to see if life on the other side of the commitment fence is better or worse than where they are currently. So take time to imagine the picture of society lived Jesus' way as an attempt to demonstrate the power of his love and commands. In considering this kind of a world, they should realize that trading in their current life for one lived Jesus' way has fantastic personal and cultural advantages.

REALITY CHECK

Regardless of where people are spiritually, most want to make a positive impact on our society. By the end of this discussion, Christian group members should be motivated to love all kinds of people (even those they don't like or feel comfortable with initially) with an irrational, unselfish love. It's the only way to obey the commands of Christ. Those who are not yet followers of Jesus should understand just how high of a bar Jesus has set for a lifestyle of radical love.

At the end of this Reality Check portion, challenge everyone in the group to carry out an experiment over the next week: Act with the love of Jesus. If they do so, there's no doubt that some in the group—and those on the receiving end of kindnesses too—will be even more attracted to Jesus!

CONCLUSION

A SURPRISING PENALTY

At certain junctures in the life of your group, you'll want to use a tool to clarify the main story of Jesus' life and the central reason for his visit to planet Earth. "A Surprising Penalty" section will help you at these junctures. It's a tool designed to be versatile enough to be used in a variety of circumstances:

- If a person is frustrated at the emptiness of living a life disconnected from God, you may want to point him to read it on his own.
- If they ask what the main message of Christianity is, it may be better to sit down and discuss it together (you can read it out loud together or silently—whatever feels most comfortable—and then discuss it).
- It might serve as a great answer to a question that comes up during group time or one-on-one conversation after the group meeting.

Read "A Surprising Penalty" carefully and use it strategically as the relational opportunities arise to discuss how Jesus' life and death intersect the lives of your group members. Be sure that you understand the nature of this story and how it relates to the story of Jesus' life. Then help your group members understand it. If they are interested in making the "ABC" commitment, be sure to let them know that their first step is to talk to God about it. Offer to pray with them. It may become a conversation that changes their life . . . and eternity!

ACKNOWLEDGMENTS

I am bursting with gratitude to all who made these guides possible. So many people have contributed to this project that it would be impossible to thank them all. However, some who have made an exceptionally large contribution rightfully deserve to be acknowledged.

Thanks to Garry Poole and Mark Mittelberg for opening the doors for these guides to be published. Tim Anstead was a great asset in web research. Hundreds of leaders field tested the material in earlier forms and gave great feedback. InterVarsity at the University of Illinois pioneered new ideas, tools, and strategies. Willow Creek has provided an entirely new platform for the Reality Check series to be utilized. My dream editor, Ramona Tucker, took these guides to an entirely new level with passion and professionalism. Most of all, I'd like to thank Kelle Ashton for bearing the weight of extra home duties, putting up with scores of late nights, and believing in me—long before anyone else did.

Thank you all!

Willow Creek Association
Vision, Training, Resources for Prevailing Churches

This resource was created to serve you and to help you in building a local church that prevails!

Since 1992, the Willow Creek Association (WCA) has been linking like-minded, action-oriented churches with each other and with strategic vision, training, and resources. Now a worldwide network of over 6,400 churches from more than ninety denominations, the WCA works to equip Member Churches and others with the tools needed to build prevailing churches. Our desire is to inspire, equip, and encourage Christian leaders to build biblically functioning churches that reach increasing numbers of unchurched people, not just with innovations from Willow Creek Community Church in South Barrington, Illinois, but from any church in the world that has experienced God-given breakthroughs.

WILLOW CREEK CONFERENCES

Each year, thousands of local church leaders, staff and volunteers—from WCA Member Churches and others—attend one of our conferences or training events. Conferences offered on the Willow Creek campus in South Barrington, Illinois, include:

Prevailing Church Conference: Foundational training for staff and volunteers working to build a prevailing local church.

Prevailing Church Workshops: More than fifty strategic, day-long workshops covering seven topic areas that represent key characteristics of a prevailing church; offered twice each year.

Promiseland Conference: Children's ministries; infant through fifth grade.

Student Ministries Conference: Junior and senior high ministries.

Willow Creek Arts Conference: Vision and training for Christian artists using their gifts in the ministries of local churches.

Leadership Summit: Envisioning and equipping Christians with leadership gifts and responsibilities; broadcast live via satellite to eighteen cities across North America.

Contagious Evangelism Conference: Encouragement and training for churches and church leaders who want to be strategic in reaching lost people for Christ.

Small Groups Conference: Exploring how developing a church *of* small groups can play a vital role in developing authentic Christian community that leads to spiritual transformation.

To find out more about WCA conferences, visit our website at www.willowcreek.com.

PREVAILING CHURCH REGIONAL WORKSHOPS

Each year the WCA team leads several, two-day training events in select cities across the United States. Some twenty day-long workshops are offered in topic areas including leadership, next-generation ministries, small groups, arts and worship, evangelism, spiritual gifts, financial stewardship, and spiritual formation. These events make quality training more accessible and affordable to larger groups of staff and volunteers.

To find out more about Prevailing Church Regional Workshops, visit our website at www.willowcreek.com.

WILLOW CREEK RESOURCES™

Churches can look to Willow Creek Resources™ for a trusted channel of ministry tools in areas of leadership, evangelism, spiritual gifts, small groups, drama, contemporary music, financial stewardship, spiritual transformation, and more. For ordering information, call (800) 570-9812 or visit our website at www.willowcreek.com.

WCA MEMBERSHIP

Membership in the Willow Creek Association as well as attendance at WCA Conferences is for churches, ministries, and leaders who hold to a historic, orthodox understanding of biblical Christianity. The annual church membership fee of $249 provides substantial discounts for your entire team on all conferences and Willow Creek Resources, networking opportunities with other outreach-oriented churches, a bimonthly newsletter, a subscription to the *Defining Moments* monthly audio journal for leaders, and more.

To find out more about WCA membership, visit our website at www.willowcreek.com.

WILLOWNET (WWW.WILLOWCREEK.COM)

This Internet resource service provides access to hundreds of Willow Creek messages, drama scripts, songs, videos, and multimedia ideas. The system allows you to sort through these elements and download them for a fee.

Our website also provides detailed information on the Willow Creek Association, Willow Creek Community Church, WCA membership, conferences, training events, resources, and more.

WILLOWCHARTS.COM (WWW.WILLOWCHARTS.COM)

Designed for local church worship leaders and musicians, WillowCharts.com provides online access to hundreds of music charts and chart components, including choir, orchestral, and horn sections, as well as rehearsal tracks and video streaming of Willow Creek Community Church performances.

THE NET (HTTP://STUDENTMINISTRY.WILLOWCREEK.COM)

The NET is an online training and resource center designed by and for student ministry leaders. It provides an inside look at the structure, vision, and mission of prevailing student ministries from around the world. The NET gives leaders access to complete programming elements, including message outlines, dramas, small group questions, and more. An indispensable resource and networking tool for prevailing student ministry leaders!

CONTACT THE WILLOW CREEK ASSOCIATION

If you have comments or questions, or would like to find out more about WCA events or resources, please contact us:

Willow Creek Association
P.O. Box 3188, Barrington, IL 60011-3188
Phone: (800) 570-9812 or (847) 765-0070
Fax (888) 922-0035 or (847) 765-5046
Web: www.willowcreek.com

REALITY CHECK SERIES
by Mark Ashton

Winning at Life
Learn the secrets Jesus taught his disciples about winning at life through the stories he told.
Saddle Stitch
ISBN: 0-310-24525-7

Jesus' Greatest Moments
Uncover the facts and meaning of the provocative events of the final week of Jesus' life.
Saddle Stitch
ISBN: 0-310-24528-1

Leadership Jesus Style
Learn the leadership principles taught and lived by Jesus.
Saddle Stitch
ISBN: 0-310-24526-5

Hot Issues
Find out how Jesus addressed the challenges of racism, feminism, sexuality, materialism, poverty, and intolerance.
Saddle Stitch
ISBN: 0-310-24523-0

When Tragedy Strikes
Discover Jesus' perspective on the problem of suffering and evil in the world.
Saddle Stitch
ISBN: 0-310-24524-9

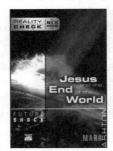

Future Shock
Uncover Jesus' perspective on the mysteries of the future as revealed in the Bible.
Saddle Stitch
ISBN: 0-310-24527-3

Sudden Impact
Discover the life-changing power of Jesus as he interacted with his contemporaries.
Saddle Stitch
ISBN: 0-310-24522-2

Clear Evidence
Weigh the arguments for and against the Jesus of the Bible.
Saddle Stitch
ISBN: 0-310-24746-2

www.zondervan.com/realitycheckcentral.org

ZONDERVAN™

GRAND RAPIDS, MICHIGAN 49530 USA
WWW.ZONDERVAN.COM

WILLOW CREEK
RESOURCES
www.willowcreek.com

Tackle the Tough Questions

Tough Questions Series

By Garry Poole and Judson Poling

Foreword by Lee Strobel

Tough questions. Reasonable questions. The kinds of questions that require informed and satisfying answers to challenges against the Christian faith.

Each guide within the **Tough Questions Series** spends six sessions dealing frankly with a specific question that seekers and believers often ask about Christianity. These thought-provoking discussions will help your group find answers and discover how reasonable the Christian faith really is.

Question 1: How Does Anyone Know God Exists?   ISBN: 0-310-22225-7
Question 2: Is Jesus the Only Way?   ISBN: 0-310-22231-1
Question 3: How Reliable Is the Bible?   ISBN: 0-310-22226-5
Question 4: How Could God Allow Suffering and Evil?   ISBN: 0-310-22227-3
Question 5: Don't All Religions Lead to God?   ISBN: 0-310-22229-X
Question 6: Do Science and the Bible Conflict?   ISBN: 0-310-22232-X
Question 7: Why Become a Christian?   ISBN: 0-310-22228-1
Tough Questions Leader's Guide   ISBN: 0-310-22224-9

Look for the **Tough Questions Series** *at your local Christian bookstore.*

ZONDERVAN™

GRAND RAPIDS, MICHIGAN 49530 USA

WWW.ZONDERVAN.COM

WILLOW CREEK

RESOURCES

www.willowcreek.com

The Case for Christ

Lee Strobel

Is Jesus really the divine Son of God? What reason is there to believe that he is?

In this best-seller, investigative reporter Lee Strobel examines the claims of Christ. Written in the style of a block-buster investigative report, *The Case for Christ* puts the toughest questions about Christ to experts in the fields of science, psychology, law, medicine, biblical studies, and more.

The result is a powerful narrative that will convince seekers and believers alike of the proven reality of Jesus Christ.

"Lee Strobel asks the questions a tough-minded skeptic would ask. Every inquirer should have it."

—Phillip E. Johnson, law professor, University of California at Berkeley

Hardcover	ISBN: 0-310-22646-5
Softcover	ISBN: 0-310-20930-7
Evangelism Pack	ISBN: 0-310-22605-8
Mass Market 6-pack	ISBN: 0-310-22627-9
Abridged Audio Pages® cassette	ISBN: 0-310-21960-4
Unabridged Audio Pages® cassette	ISBN: 0-310-24825-6
Unabridged Audio Pages® CD	ISBN: 0-310-24779-9
Student Edition	ISBN: 0-310-23484-0
Student Edition 6-pack (with Leader's Guide)	ISBN: 0-310-24851-5

Pick up a copy today at your favorite bookstore!

ZONDERVAN™

GRAND RAPIDS, MICHIGAN 49530 USA

WWW.ZONDERVAN.COM

WILLOW CREEK RESOURCES

www.willowcreek.com

The Case for Faith

Lee Strobel

Was God telling the truth when he said, "You will seek me and find me when you seek me with all your heart"?

In his best-seller *The Case for Christ,* the legally trained investigative reporter Lee Strobel examined the claims of Christ, reaching the hard-won yet satisfying verdict that Jesus is God's unique Son.

But despite the compelling historical evidence that Strobel presented, many grapple with doubts or serious concerns about faith in God. As in a court of law, they want to shout, "Objection!" They say, "If God is love, then what about all of the suffering that festers in our world?" Or, "If Jesus is the door to heaven, then what about the millions who have never heard of him?"

In *The Case for Faith,* Strobel turns his tenacious investigative skills to the most persistent emotional objections to belief, the eight "heart" barriers to faith. *The Case for Faith* is for those who may be feeling attracted to Jesus but who are faced with formidable intellectual barriers standing squarely in their path. For Christians, it will deepen their convictions and give them fresh confidence in discussing Christianity with even their most skeptical friends.

Hardcover	ISBN: 0-310-22015-7
Softcover	ISBN: 0-310-23469-7
Evangelism Pack	ISBN: 0-310-23508-1
Mass Market 6-pack	ISBN: 0-310-23509-X
Abridged Audio Pages® cassette	ISBN: 0-310-23475-1
Unabridged Audio Pages® cassette	ISBN: 0-310-24825-6
Unabridged Audio Pages® CD	ISBN: 0-310-24787-X
Student Edition	ISBN: 0-310-24188-X
Student Edition 6-pack (with Leader's Guide)	ISBN: 0-310-24922-8

Pick up a copy today at your favorite bookstore!

ZONDERVAN™

GRAND RAPIDS, MICHIGAN 49530 USA

WWW.ZONDERVAN.COM

WILLOW CREEK
RESOURCES

www.willowcreek.com

A Bible for Seeking God and Understanding Life

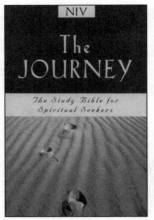

New International Version

The Journey

The Journey is uniquely designed to help spiritual seekers discover the practical aspects of Christianity—and better understand God. Notes and insights are woven throughout the complete NIV Bible text and address key questions seekers are asking about the Bible and its relevance today.

With helpful features like icon-tagged information windows, introductory articles, and reading plans, *The Journey* lets you explore a number of themes:

- **Discovering God**—Addresses the many aspect of God's Character.
- **Addressing Questions**—Deals with some of your toughest questions.
- **Strengthening Relationships**—Focuses on marriage, parenting, leadership, and social relationships.
- **Reasons to Believe**—Answers the question, "Why should I believe?"
- **Knowing Yourself**—Helps you look at your own identity in the light of God's word.
- **Managing Resources**—Uncovers the Bible's most practical aspects.

Softcover	ISBN: 0-310-92023-X
Gospel of John	ISBN: 0-310-91951-7

Pick up a copy today at your favorite bookstore!

ZONDERVAN™

GRAND RAPIDS, MICHIGAN 49530 USA

WWW.ZONDERVAN.COM

WILLOW CREEK RESOURCES

www.willowcreek.com

Christianity 101
Your Guide to Eight Basic Christian Beliefs

You Mean to Say You Don't Know the
Meaning of:

- Monophysitism?
- Hypostatic Union?
- Infralapsarian?
- Traducianism?
- Chiliastic?
- Pneumatomachian?

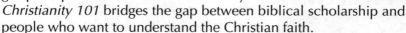

Cheer up! You don't have to have a
thousand-dollar vocabulary in order to
grasp the priceless basics of Christianity.
Christianity 101 bridges the gap between biblical scholarship and
people who want to understand the Christian faith.

This book presents eight basic doctrines of Christianity—The
Bible, God, Christ, Holy Spirit, Human Beings, Redemption, The
Church, and The Last Things—in clear, simple language that gives
seasoned Christians a fresh understanding of the Bible and its
teachings and puts new Christians on familiar terms with Christian
doctrine. Gilbert Bilezikian does not shape his analysis of these
doctrines in the worn-out, rationalistic categories of older system-
atic theologies, but in vibrant, dynamic language designed to com-
municate biblical truths to contemporary believers.

Softcover   ISBN: 0-310-57701-2

Pick up a copy today at your favorite bookstore!

ZONDERVAN™

GRAND RAPIDS, MICHIGAN 49530 USA

WWW.ZONDERVAN.COM

WILLOW CREEK
RESOURCES

www.willowcreek.com

Building a Church of Small Groups
A Place Where Nobody Stands Alone

Bill Donahue and Russ Robinson

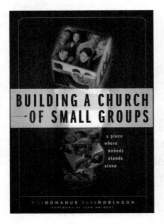

How can church become a place where nobody stands alone? Through small groups! Like nothing else, they provide the kind of life-giving community that builds and empowers the body of Christ and impacts the world. At Willow Creek Community Church, small groups are so important that they define the core organizational strategy. Bill Donahue and Russ Robinson write, "We have gone from a church *with* small groups . . . to being a church *of* small groups."

Building a Church of Small Groups unpacks the:

- vision
- values
- strategies required to integrate small groups into your entire ministry

Hardcover   ISBN: 0-310-24035-2

Pick up a copy today at your favorite bookstore!

GRAND RAPIDS, MICHIGAN 49530 USA
WWW.ZONDERVAN.COM

www.willowcreek.com

Now in a Revised Edition

Leading Life-Changing Small Groups

Bill Donahue

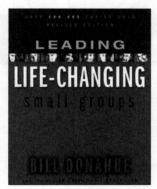

Like nothing else, small groups have the power to change lives. They're the ideal route to discipleship, a place where the rubber of biblical truth meets the road of human relations.

As director of adult education and training at Willow Creek Community Church, Bill Donahue knows that small groups are key to building biblical community and thriving individuals. In *Leading Life-Changing Small Groups,* Donahue and his team share in-depth the practical insights that have made Willow Creek's small group ministry so incredibly effective.

Softcover   ISBN: 0-310-24750-0

Pick up a copy today at your favorite bookstore!

ZONDERVAN™

GRAND RAPIDS, MICHIGAN 49530 USA

WWW.ZONDERVAN.COM

WILLOW CREEK

RESOURCES

www.willowcreek.com

Continue the Transformation

Pursuing Spiritual Transformation Series

John Ortberg, Laurie Pederson, and Judson Poling

Experience a radical change in how you think and how you live. Forget about trying hard to be a better person. Welcome instead to the richly rewarding process of discovering and growing into the person God made you to be! Developed by Willow Creek Community Church as its core curriculum, this planned, progressive small group approach to spiritual maturity will help you:

- Become more like Jesus
- Recapture the image of God in your life
- Cultivate intimacy with God
- Live your faith everywhere, all the time
- Renew your zest for life

Leader's guide included!

Fully Devoted: Living Each Day in Jesus' Name	ISBN: 0-310-22073-4
Grace: An Invitation to a Way of Life	ISBN: 0-310-22074-2
Growth: Training vs. Trying	ISBN: 0-310-22075-0
Groups: The Life-Giving Power of Community	ISBN: 0-310-22076-9
Gifts: The Joy of Serving God	ISBN: 0-310-22077-7
Giving: Unlocking the Heart of Good Stewardship	ISBN: 0-310-22078-5

*Look for **Pursuing Spiritual Transformation** at your local Christian bookstore.*

ZONDERVAN™

GRAND RAPIDS, MICHIGAN 49530 USA

WWW.ZONDERVAN.COM

WILLOW CREEK

RESOURCES

www.willowcreek.com

Continue Building Your New Community!

New Community Series

Bill Hybels and John Ortberg
With Kevin and Sherry Harney

If you appreciate not having to choose between Bible study and building community, then you'll want to explore all eight New Community Bible study guides. Delve deeply into Scripture in a way that strengthens relationships. Challenging questions will encourage your group members to reflect not only on Scripture but also on the old idea of community done in a new, culturally relevant way.

Each guide contains six transforming sessions—filled with prayer, insight, intimacy, and action—to help your small group members line up their lives and relationships more closely with the Bible's model for the church.

Exodus: Journey Toward God — ISBN: 0-310-22771-2
Parables: Imagine Life God's Way — ISBN: 0-310-22881-6
Sermon on the Mount[1]: Connect with God — ISBN: 0-310-22883-2
Sermon on the Mount[2]: Connect with Others — ISBN: 0-310-22884-0
Acts: Rediscover Church — ISBN: 0-310-22770-4
Romans: Find Freedom — ISBN: 0-310-22765-8
Philippians: Run the Race — ISBN: 0-310-23314-3
Colossians: A Whole New You — ISBN: 0-310-22769-0
James: Live Wisely — ISBN: 0-310-22767-4
1 Peter: Stand Strong — ISBN: 0-310-22773-9
1 John: Love Each Other — ISBN: 0-310-22768-2
Revelation: Experience God's Power — ISBN: 0-310-22882-4

Look for New Community at your local Christian bookstore or by calling 800-727-3480.

ZONDERVAN™

GRAND RAPIDS, MICHIGAN 49530 USA

WWW.ZONDERVAN.COM

www.willowcreek.com

Mark Ashton is the director of seeker small groups at Willow Creek Community Church. In addition, Mark supervises the staff for more than forty new believers groups and Willow's Internationals ministry. He is also the director of *TruthQuest*—Willow's ministry that answers tough questions about Jesus and Christianity. Mark is a frequent speaker at conferences and is the author of *Absolute Truth?*

For more information, go to
www.zondervan.com/realitycheckcentral.org.

We want to hear from you. Please send your comments about this book to us in care of the address below. Thank you.

GRAND RAPIDS, MICHIGAN 49530 USA
WWW.ZONDERVAN.COM